# THE WILD WEST WIND
## REMEMBERING ALLEN GINSBERG

OTHER BOOKS AND BROADSIDES
BY SUSAN EDWARDS

*Day of the Dead Zodiac*
*Song to Beseech the Ancestors*
*Blessed Mother Not Afraid of Snakes*
*The Samadhi of the Guru*
*The Heretic Valentine*

# THE WILD WEST WIND
## REMEMBERING ALLEN GINSBERG

### SUSAN EDWARDS

BAKSUN BOOKS

THE PRACTICAL MYSTIC

This piece first appeared in WOMAN & PERFORMANCE/ A Journal of Feminist Theory,
"Performing Autobiography"
Vol. 10:1-2, #19-20 1999.
New York University, Tisch School of the Arts,
Department of Performance Studies

## THE WILD WEST WIND/ Remembering Allen Ginsberg

Text and illustrations © Susan Edwards 1999
Introduction © C. Carr 2000
Tyger, drawing by Allen Ginsberg 1992
Includes bibliographic references and notes
ISBN #1-887997-19-9

1. Allen Ginsberg  2. Memoir  3. Buddhism  4. Women's Studies

The
Practical
Mystic

Published in the United States by
Baksun Books
1838 Pine Street
Boulder, Colorado 80302
with
The Practical Mystic
1107 Cedar Avenue
Boulder, Colorado 80304

Funded in part by the
Boulder Arts Commission, City of Boulder and
AHAB The Arts and Humanities Assembly of Boulder County through an AHAB/Addison Mini-Grant

*For my teachers, living and otherwise*

I'm beginning to think he's a great saint,
a great saint concealed in a veneer of demonism.

—Jack Kerouac, on Allen Ginsberg

...No more sweet summers with lovers, teaching Blake at Naropa.

—Allen Ginsberg, last poem

# INTRODUCTION

The Beats were the first bohemian movement born under the eye of mass media, and the man at the center of that movement became our first celebrity poet, disdained and admired for all the wrong reasons. Some would dismiss Allen Ginsberg as a bearded bathless Beat, the ultimate commie pinko queer. Others saw him as a star, the bard who could hobnob with any Hollywood Square.

Over the years, I felt introduced to a more human Ginsberg through my friend Susan's perceptions of both his strengths and his flaws. Susan Edwards and I made our first treks to Boulder in 1976, though that year our paths crossed there for just a day. As I recall, we spent part of that time disemboweling the Disembodied School. I was having trouble with the poets. Some seemed less interested in teaching than in their own self-importance, and the competitiveness among my fellow students went beyond the sniper fire found in most writing classes. So much ego on display. I am no Buddhist and found this ironic.

Ginsberg had not yet arrived, though, since his father was recently dead. "The Beat thing is a disguise," Susan told me. "He's really a scholar." I still remember his class, and how I appreciated it because he actually taught literature. Still, I had to adjust my attitude, because I was expecting some kind of "Beat" experience, at least on the first day. Instead, he described reading Wordsworth's *Intimations of Immortality* to his dying father. While Ginsberg told us that he thought Wordsworth was straining for a visionary experience, I couldn't believe that the author of *Howl* and *Kaddish* was expounding on a poet so hoary and dull. But he went on to discuss Wordsworth with such passion and insight that I left class wanting to reread him.

Susan's proposed hagiography is warts-and-all, written with love. Her observations about gender, Ginsberg's attitude towards women, are especially valuable, since few seem willing to discuss this topic. (I doubt that Ginsberg himself would be so squeamish.) One day in class, he announced that he—and Whitman, his great predecessor—both considered women an afterthought. So. One more practitioner in the ignore-the-women lineage. I didn't much care, since his generosity as a teacher applied to everyone. I also never felt undermined by him, as I did in certain other classes where my lack of genius quickly became apparent.

I think the last time I heard him read was here in New York at a squatters' benefit in some dingy Loisaida crawl space early in the 1990s. Ginsberg enjoyed his fame, but he certainly didn't need to make appearances like that one. He just never lost his sense of mission.

Ginsberg was a great American bard because he saw the poetry in madness, ugliness, and struggle. And it took real heart to see it there. He really was a pinko queer—antiwar, antinuke and early out of the closet. But I think that self-assigned activism, that sense of duty to the world, really came to fruition in Ginsberg's adopted hometown of Boulder. There, as Susan makes clear, he was constantly giving of himself, whether he was playing parent to irascible old buddies or co-founding a school named after one of them. What he hoped to transmit at The Jack Kerouac School of Disembodied Poetics was, he said, "beatnik ecstasy chastened by classic meditation." The fact that he wanted to instruct those who came after him, not just by teaching a class here or there but by establishing a certain path to follow, really sets him apart as a literary figure.

C. Carr
New York City
May 2000

*It soared, a bird, it held its flight, a swift pure cry, soar silver orb it leaped serene, speeding, sustained, to come, don't spin it out too long long breath the breath long life, soaring high, high resplendent, aflame, crowned, high in the effulgence symbolistic, high, of the ethereal bosom, high, of the high vast irradiation everywhere all soaring all around about the all, the needlessnessnessness...*

—James Joyce

*ULYSSES*

AHHHHH fills the room creaking through his vocal cords grown crusty with time and longing.

Now he is gone.

Allen Ginsberg's chutzpah when confronted with the insurmountable propels me to describe and perhaps elucidate a small portion of his life and times as experienced by his "old collaborator," a title he bestowed on me the last time I saw him, he sitting under the Naropa trees, our hands entwined, our eyes locked by a too-long absence. This memoir will travel from the New World to Rome where, strange as it might seem, I, at last, got wind of Allen Ginsberg.

His life and work is autobiography in its largest sense. Allen was not capable of making it up. He was too busy living and documenting it to waste time on fiction. Rather than "autobiography," maybe his life work should be considered Poetic Non-fiction. His life was lived as a bardic spokesman and participant in His Times/Our Times. Like Dante, he wrote his own Comedy while remaining the ever-observant, ever-eager pilgrim.

While Allen was jet-setting around the world reading his poetry, establishing himself as a Major Poet, and fighting for the free speech of poets everywhere, our bodily connection existed solely during his Rocky Mountain sojourns in Boulder, Colorado. The Buddhist capital that drew him here has since transmigrated to Nova Scotia, Canada. Allen, too, has transmigrated. In those days of yore, Allen set up shop in this small university town where he determined to co-found, build and defend with Anne Waldman—his ally, friend, fellow poet, "fast speaking woman"—The Jack Kerouac School of Disembodied Poetics at The Naropa Institute (now Naropa University), founded by Chögyam Trungpa Rinpoche.[1]

Early on, Allen told me that he was going to adopt the Buddhist practice of *darshan* as his teaching style. *Darshan* is a Sanskrit word that describes how the student learns by being around their teachers, in proximity, by watching what their teachers do and how they go about doing it. Allen took this as his model both for applying Buddhist teachings to daily life and working with aspiring young poets who flocked to Naropa. Through the tremendous force and skill of his personality, a force often as gentle as it was bombastic, his influence was to extend not just to students but to his entire poetry community and beyond to include the international arena of arts and politics.

But Boulder was the context in which I knew Allen. Like Allen, I too heard voices and an inner voice told me to help Anne and Allen build their school. From those early raw days in the mid-1970s to the more mature, established days of the late 1980s up until the beginning of the 1990s, I worked and played next to him in the sparkling and caustic sphere of influence generated both by his stature as a major American poet and his willingness to be a simple student of ancient teachings both Buddhist and literary. You could not really know Allen without finding yourself part of the story, part of the performance, part of the pact to make it new: an American life worth living, a spiritual path worth following.

Now he is gone. His life, an epic written largely by his own hand, spoken by his own voice, young and old, tasted and felt by a body full of sexual honesty and bravado, is what we have to go on. Though I would not describe his style as "self-mythologizing," as some have, his life was lived with relentless self-awareness.[2]

Allen saw his life as part of a continuity of bardic yogis who might liberate the world with the right word spoken at the right time as he had experienced when he orated *Howl* at the Six Gallery, San Francisco, in 1955. His words arose from his sympathies for those

> who fell on their knees in hopeless cathedrals praying for each other's salva-
> tion and light and breasts, until the soul illuminated its hair for a
> second...[3]

He, surprised to be holding the keys to the poetry kingdom, opened the gates of heaven and fame with his words and connected to his Poetic Soul Buddies, the long-forgotten 18th century poet Christopher Smart, precursor to the visionary William Blake and the American man-lover, Walt Whitman. He shared that lineage in the here and now of the 1950s with Jack Kerouac, William S. Burroughs, Gregory Corso, Gary Snyder, Lawrence Ferlinghetti, Michael McClure, Diane di Prima and handfuls of simpaticos.

Flatirous - Boulder - Colorado. USA

If you were around him from those days on, you touched the raw nerve of the story line: an original amalgam of Whitman's request for "perfect personal candor," mind breaths, liberation theologico-poetico-passion and expertise performed in public and private. It could shake you to the marrow and melt and transmute the lead of cynicism that had been injected into your American heart: "America I'm putting my queer shoulder to the wheel."[4]

Allen's life refuses to follow the protocols of evidence. Perhaps, rather than squeeze his life into the restrictions of the standard autobiographical container, we should resort to simple hagiography, words written for the holy. Allen's life activity qualifies him as one worthy of this consideration. He was a visionary, an urban mendicant. He never denied but proclaimed the spiritual basis of his art; he established and protected his poetry community; he nudged the constricted sphincter of academe and opened rusty bardic gates with a flurry of human rights enthusiasm. He could be a cardinal, a rabbi, a roshi. Saint Ginzy, the first Jewish saint of America. He cajoled, berated and inspired writing students to see writing as a path to mind-liberation, a way to work with suffering and brilliance all at once.

To make our petition for Allen's sainthood more complex, gender must be considered—though his gender style, too, does not fit into the current paradigm. In the midst of his successful male posturing and accomplishment, he was a man who continually surrendered. He put other men and their needs/works before himself, served them even in the midst of the seductions of his own fame and notoriety. At the end of his life, he was still raising money for Naropa, the child of his mind and the sweat of his body.

The last time I saw
Allen he was sitting
alone on a folding
chair under
a Naropa tree

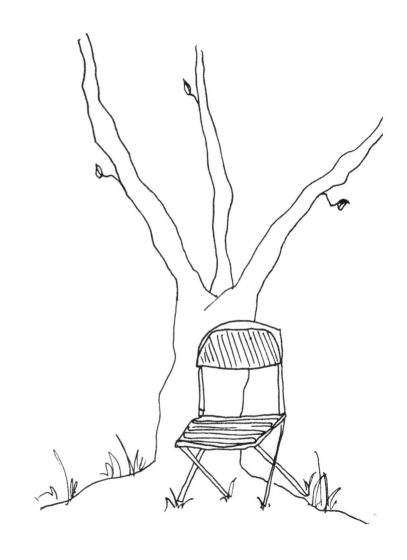

At times he thought he might be masochistic, but it was his character, his nature to accommodate his community in ways that a woman at the fin de siècle might find abhorrent.

On the one hand, he would proclaim pompously, "I want to be known as the most brilliant man in America"—if only for a moment. In the next second, like a mother, he nurtured and buttressed. It was especially for his poetry buddies that he showed his maternal bond. One evening, after Gregory Corso had continually disrupted an event with his booming taunts, Allen turned to me and said, "You know, I can't tolerate his behavior. I only do it because he's a great poet and I love him." This followed Corso's taunting Allen with unruly bellows of "Momma Ginzy! Momma Ginzy!"

On another occasion, during the Kerouac Conference in 1982, he insisted that the artist, Karl Appel, who was fashioning an enormous painting based on a famous photo of Kerouac, include the crucifix that Jack was wearing at the original photoshoot. It had been airbrushed away when it first appeared in a national publication. Allen was going to set things aright. He was in continuous relationship with comrades alive or dead: they were the essentials of the Ginsberg canon. The Lone Cowboy wasn't an option. Like an accomplished courtesan, he wasn't afraid of male power, beauty and technical skill but served them and accepted his own success with a modicum of excitement. One hot summer day he told me that he was now an historical personage. "It doesn't matter what I do anymore. It's already done. I'm tired of writing. Think I'll spend some time doing my photography." He was neither happy nor sad about his achievement. Of course, he continued to write.

Allen · Anne · Gregory
in the 1970s
The Age of Hair

Quick as Jack Flash, he could jump from all-repentant feminine accommodation to his marrow-deep long-ing to be part of the lineage of great writers and great teachers. He wanted to be one of the Dead White Males. He won't qualify. The FCC continues to censor the reading of his work on radio during prime listening hours and the Tweed Suits seem loathe to accept a Jewish Buddhist faggot's contribution to American letters.[5] Allen wanted to be part of it all. If Raphael and he had been contemporaries, he would have asked him to paint his portrait in among those in the artists' fresco, *Parnassus*, maybe next to Dante. On the other hand, Allen would just as easily have offered the portrait to Burroughs or Kerouac. He cared and he didn't. Moreover, *The School of Athens,* fresco of philosophers, might be a more appropriate venue for his questing and classical spirit, his longing for the sacred conversation.

He sought a hallowed place among the immortals because it was a place of genuine meaning and signif-icance for him. It was a place to humbly offer himself, to bring the honor and splendor of words well spoken, to make homage to the ancestors, to dedicate himself to the craft, to embody the love of the human experiment, to enjoy rapport with those who went before, to listen to the soul music of the pres-ent moment, to the heart-pounding speculations about truth, the politics of the-condition-human, the body beautiful and male. Allen lived on the cutting edge but he was "classical" in his perceptions.

Allen & Blake supplant Plato & Aristotle in "The School of Athens."

Allen's sexuality is not going to attract or endear him to the oh-so-quickly-codified current of contemporary queer studies. He wasn't an ideologue about queerness, only about the right to love whom you love—even if it was a boy. Of course, Allen preferred straight men so he was never in a "gay" community *per se*. We often laughed about that, about what a "real" woman he was, always on the lookout for a hunk. He would do anything for a masculine, straight guy, including giving away his money and his patience, especially if the hunk was a good poet. In an incredible moment of male bonding, Allen forgave Ezra Pound his anti-Semitism because Allen considered Pound's superb tracking of the mind more important than a single example of "fucked up" thinking. This when Pound himself acknowledged his "stupid suburban prejudice."[6] Allen wanted Pound's Poet-Blessing, not his contrition.

It was another thing to be a woman in his world. Receptive as he was, he was the man. And he was the Head Man. Many of his women students found him patronizing, irritating and finally just an old man with nothing new to say. He found them maudlin and too emotional. Not bone tough and full of sweaty details. Ironically, his own sometimes desperate passion for the literal made good poetry, but it was as though he was fighting his own visionary nature, his own abstractions, his own dreams in order to support, to concede to consensual reality. He would shout and sometimes vigorously stamp his feet, "What EXACTLY is happening in this poem?"

Allen had dreams, although they would never manifest as the *bête noir* Burroughs confronted. He saw and felt the suffering of life but worked carefully to keep his spiritual nature from exuding saccharin sentiment. A small example is the change he made in the first line of *Howl*: "mystical" becomes "hysterical" to make it grittier. A larger, more complicated example is how, for Ezra Pound's 82nd birthday in 1967, Allen chanted the Buddhist Three Vows:[7]

*Buddham Saranam Gochamee*

*Dhamam Saranam Gochamee*

*Sangham Saranam Gochamee*

Pound was in a self-loathing and depressive state. Allen—Momma Ginzy—was giving Pound the only remedy and comfort he had to give. He made no explanation. He might not have had one in 1967. In later years, Allen made much of the decades of the 20th century. He often taught his ill-informed students 20th-century history broken into decades and his personal involvement in the issues. The decade of the 1960s were especially a time of seeking teachings from afar. He also implicitly trusted Kerouac's 1950s immersion in the Buddhist teachings. Seeds were taking root for Allen.

This toughness and fear of gushy sentiment—Blake was never gushy—made Allen's relationship with women difficult. He seldom helped women make the transition from what he considered to be sappy autobiographical/confessional writing to literal observations full of snappy details without insulting them. The tenuousness of women's place in the world, the lack of a colorful, seminal, earth-shaking lineage, made him nervous and impatient.

In my own experience with him, he would shout, "You're too sensitive!" I learned to stay out of the way of his proclamations and judgments. The possibility of him shouting at me as he did to others, "Make it great!" sent shivers of revulsion and terror through me. Once he asked me, after reading a piece of mine, whether I was insane. After that, I always cautioned women students to take his feedback with a grain of salt. Or if he thought you insane, I told them, it might be confirmation of a good piece of writing.

Insanity was a shadow world of women's sensibility that followed and haunted him. Perhaps because of his mother's madness he wasn't able to accept with grace the voice of women—unless they accepted the parameters of a world described by Real Men—even if those men dwelt on the queer margins. Simply put, women's experience, women's Otherness, was too threatening to his fearsome determination to connect to the Real World. Women, as far as he could see, weren't even in the conversation (although later in life he attempted to correct that). One might have to concede that he was the best and most dedicated traditional woman among us, but he knew how to butch it up for the sake of an audience and in the real world it helped to have male hormones.

Allen was a faggot who wrote of manly things: the world, visions, politics, spirituality, sex, power, the truth of mind. A woman doing that just wasn't going to be an equal to him, although he did consider Diane di Prima and Anne Waldman to be poetic geniuses. Maybe they were the only two.

In our century, he spoke to and for his "beatific" generation (Ginsberg's "third" Kerouacian definition of beat: "the necessary beatness or darkness that precedes opening up to light, egolessness, giving room for religious illumination"[8]) and the ones that followed, as well as the urban poor, the ozone hole, censorship, free love, freedom of expression, political abuses and great poetry. His story is an epic, a Roman orgy led by a humble Jewish faggot from New Jersey. Allen knew America was beautiful.

When I first met Allen in Boulder, his career was taking off. He was almost 50. He still had time to party back in the mid-1970s, but as the stunning success of the Jack Kerouac Conference in 1982 made evident, the rest of his life would be one of dedicated and continually expanding service to his community of writers, bards, geniuses and men who loved men. He worked to near exhaustion but never really complained except to note the frenzy, the passage of time, the hidden vampires of fame, the endless correspondence.

Of course, even though it was a male scene, there were women here and there. My arrival on the Boulder scene with my haiku-poetess-Zen-prodigy lover was to dovetail with his open gayness. Allen and Peter Orlovsky, Pat Donegan and I were the "out" gay couples of the conservative and homophobic Buddhist/Naropa community. We wryly noted this. A few years earlier, Allen had written me a spontaneous non-haiku. The last line: "Who's that shorthaired ghost?" He, full of energy, ink spots and eager joy, sat at a table on the grass laughing and writing. His power thundered and I leaned into it like a sailor on the deck of a rudderless ship on a storm-tossed sea. In the years that followed, Pat longed for his blessing, his respect, his mentorship. Her perseverance both as a gifted poet and as a practitioner of *darshan* eventually won Allen's professional collegial acknowledgement.[9]

To be honest, I didn't like him then and since I didn't want to be a Great Poet, the obvious hooks did not entangle me. Nor was I much drawn to his raucous crowd of Brilliant Irrepressibles. They were too much for me. If my confused alienated years in graduate school had force-fed me with ruthless New Critical exhumations of dead writers, Allen's world overwhelmed me with life and passion and alcohol and loud voices in the night. "Oy, these are the Living Poets," I would moan as I tried to sleep those hot summer nights in the Varsity Apartments, playground to The Scene.[10]

Oh what a Cool
straw hat,
And a protection Cord!
And round royal
Silver eyeglasses!

Who's that shorthaired Ghost?

— for Susan Edwards
from Allen
Ginsberg

July 6, 1977   Naropa
Inst

Now, like the flights of birds across the sky, many are gone, sonneteering among the Dead. Corso lingers on wondering whether his poetry will end up in the Beat Canon without the succor and ministrations of Momma Ginzy.[11] For months after Allen's death, Peter Orlovsky wandered the streets of New York bemoaning a confused inheritance. Anne Waldman, as co-founder of the Kerouac school, carries the torch for Allen's Naropa legacy. Allen's practice of *darshan* has begotten torchbearers all over the globe. Boulder grows more populated. Life rushes on. After Allen's death, his presence rushed back in to confuse and overwhelm me as it always has. Sitting in my attic study without him is not as much fun as when he was alive and we would argue about words and the nature of texts, giggle at ourselves and our endless demands for accomplishment, share painfully honest moments, express love deeply intuited—curious as it seemed to both of us at the time.

To return to my petition that Allen be beatified, hagiography must begin with the beginning. Allen referred to his writing career as the family business, but his poetic life burst into flame when he was reading William Blake, the 18th-century English Romantic visionary poet, painter, engraver and mystic. In his 22nd year, Allen heard Blake's voice recite three of his poems, including

> Ah Sun-flower! weary of time.
> Who countest the steps of the Sun:
> Seeking after that sweet golden clime
> Where the travellers journey is done.[12]

Allen's bardic apprenticeship to what he described as a "sacred vocation" began then and there. His mystical experience fascinated him but after fruitlessly attempting to sustain it, he chose "to shut up & live in the present temporary form."[13] He began his poetic life with a "paranormal" awakening and talked about the interplay that vision and insanity had for him to the end. It was as though his life began *in media res* of a play portraying the immemorial bloodline of wild-eyed visionary bardic geniuses, the stage cluttered with lyres and harmoniums. Since he was the living one, clearly it was his duty to continue the line, to find the way to bring the music of his complex and mystical passion into 20th-century, pragmatic, literal-minded, inarticulate America.

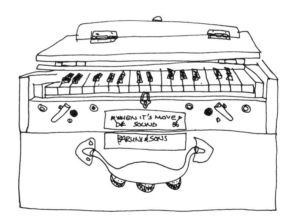

His American forefather was Walt Whitman. It was not enough for Allen that Whitman wrote of manly love between comrades. For years, Allen did considerable research to find a man he had slept with who had slept with a man who had slept with Whitman. His persistence paid off. He found the link and was ecstatic that his American pedigree also included bodily contact, bodily fluid. Allen had slept with Neal Cassidy, who had slept with Gavin Arthur (Bay Area astrologer and grandson of U. S. President Chester A. Arthur), who had slept with Edward Carpenter (a British educator-poet), who had slept with Whitman.[14] This was not a Dead Poet's Society.

Walt and Allen were also to share that long, almost breathless but buoyant line often burdened with too many words. Later, with the feedback of poets like Basil Bunting, Allen began to let the line breathe. With the mentorship of the meditation master, Chögyam Trungpa Rinpoche, Allen was encouraged to work with three-line poems. He then began to teach these guidelines to his Naropa classes: first, sink your mind into the sky, then focus back on the earth and then look inside. Allen re-committed to the spaces between words, the silence, the immediate image arising in the mind, spontaneous composition.

He had always practiced the haiku form and, as in so many areas of his life, he brought disparate and seemingly contrary worlds into harmony. Pat Donegan, in a lecture given at a Haiku Conference in Tokyo in April 1997, said Allen Ginsberg "may be the only major Western poet who used haiku as a vehicle for his life and writing, as a way to keep attentive to the moment in his daily life

Chögyam Trungpa
Rinpoche
in the 1980s
—heart's blood

whether...responding to the news of the CIA in South America or the trees of heaven swaying outside his kitchen window—and illuminated these moments in his howling words...as aptly expressed in his own haiku:"[15]

> Sunlight mixed with dust
> rises behind a truck
> on the road

The hagiography petition grows ever complicated. We need to include in the petition an argument for Allen's bardic status as Poet-Who-Brought-West-to-East. That role began when Kerouac sang the refuge prayer to him à la Frank Sinatra. Later his poetry fusions would touch his teacher. Chögyam Trungpa Rinpoche asked Allen to teach him poetics and then wrote several books of verse inspired by Allen's generosity and technical suggestions but informed by his own manifest vision of "the true nature of mind."[16]

Allen, even though he was marginalized in the larger world—at least in America where sex is still a dirty word—was unlike many artists on the margins today who simply proclaim a new territory in an attempt to avoid or deny academia altogether. Allen wanted academe to accept him even as he was hammering down the door. He wanted The Man to let him inside. He debated the neo-conservative critic, Norman Podhoretz, in his mind for decades.[17] He needed the polarity, the challenge. Finally, as a dedicated student of Buddhism, he saw the essential Wisdom of Polarity and felt deep appreciation for those who had been his real and imagined enemies. At first, one might consider polarity to be "real," the powerful seduction of Us and Them. It is our unique responses to polarities that define our character, our style as human beings. Allen aspired to "negative capability." It was John Keats's recipe for a Man of Achievement written in a December 21, 1817 letter to his brothers: "...when a man is capable of being in uncertainties, Mysteries, doubts, without any irritable reaching out after fact and reason."[18]

After many years of practice and observation of his own mind, Allen realized that he was not as alienated as he often felt but an integral part of the larger cultural conversation. He appreciated Podhoretz as a worthy opponent, which indeed he was and is. This was evident in Allen's political activities as well. During a protest at Rocky Flats Nuclear Weapons Plant in the early 1980s, Allen, amidst the hunkered protesters, made friendly conversation with grim-faced policemen. When I asked him why, he laughed and said, "Well, they're people, too. Just wearing ill-fitting blue outfits."

Still, Allen's marginality acted as a major and defining polarity in almost every aspect of his life. He was Jewish and grew up in a time when Jews abandoned their faith for the more earthly promises of Socialism. His mother was brilliant but insane. He was gay. He was smart. He was Buddhist. He was visionary.

He was angry and outspoken about injustice and greed. He challenged the government. He wanted to be accepted. He wanted to be part of history, part of literary history, part of Bardic Glory.

Allen was one of those rare artists who reach beyond the boundaries of human hierarchies to the flesh and blood of the debate. If dogma was an obstacle to the freedom to see the heart meat, he surrendered dogma, admitted when he was wrong, continued to negotiate after everyone had given up. While Allen was a maestro, a luminary, he was not interested in what might be considered mental abstractions. His experience took precedence over concepts of gender/queerness. He loved whom he loved and it is that aspect of his loving nature which will make it difficult for academia to ever accept him. By making him a saint, we accept his commitment to the path of *darshan*. We learn from his example, but it won't be sycophant to our intellectual predilections.

The relentless resistance of the margin shifted only slightly throughout his life. Although he received many honors, the highest never came his way. Where was the Nobel Prize? Wasn't his poetry spoken all over the world? Didn't he fight with courage and eloquence for human rights?

How could the Establishment accept his totality, his largeness, without revealing their own phobias and fear of his power, his gentleness, his wisdom, his skill, his integrity, his sexuality? One hopes that acceptance will come. But it will be later, when it won't embarrass anyone. When current categories expand to accommodate an artist whose work spanned most of the century and whose energies touched an international nerve center. Allen Ginsberg, America's Ambassador to the Soul Hungry.

If this were a performance, I would have to have a bearded fierce-eyed but gentle man ride in on a donkey, blow into a shofar—a ram's horn—and shatter the walls of academic/anemic/homophobic poetry. But in spite of the successes, the triumphs of Allen's orations around the world, his life and work face revisionism. Begrudgingly, it might be hauled through quickly rebuilt and re-fortified gates and refashioned into the blithering of a madman limited by drugs, the times and his perversions. Or Allen could be accepted as a lineage holder of American verse brought out of the closet into living color in the tradition of Walt Whitman. Maybe the Academy will eventually tolerate both points of view via Keatsian "negative capability" in their own scholarly practice.

On the other hand, it could be that homophobes will attempt to erase the validity of his work. Or homophiles will make him oblige their various causes. Whatever happens, we the living know that while he was alive he rode a donkey and transmogrified the staid poetry world. A world wherein academia made out the American voice to be that of an exile, the Anglophilic poet T. S. Eliot who never had the nerve or the heart to write an Anglican *kaddish* in memorium for his insane wife. (In a curious twist of fate, Eliot's poems about cats made millions on Broadway for his next, more sane wife.)

To be accepted into the hagiography, one has to transform the hard hearts of others. My own experience is a case in point. The deep and sometimes unconscious effects of Allen's practice of *darshan* begin to take effect. Something mysterious could happen when you have the opportunity to know a Great One. In spite of my efforts to keep him in "objective" perspective, Ginzy got through to me. He never held back. He always was open-minded even if he didn't agree. He loved without obvious conditions. The sheer raw power of his voice could be at times better than his poetry. He always wondered when and how I would play my cards—they were so close to my chest. When I put a few down, he flipped out but he

never gave up the debate nor the curiosity about how I was going to live my life. I watched him do this, according to the configurations of time and place, for everyone he cared about. Is this his or our autobiography?

As the final argument for my petitions, and in honor of Allen's tribute to William Carlos Williams's "no ideas but in things," let me present an example of his practice of *darshan*, autobiography and performance all at once.

Shelley awestruck in Roman Forum — palimpsest of
"The School of Athens" and millennial calligraphy

In the early years of the Summer Writing Program at Naropa, Allen gave an introductory lecture to the whole student body. A crowd of people including curious faculty collected in a large classroom (later the Tent). Allen passed out copies of Percy Bysshe Shelley's *Ode to the West Wind*.[19] He would explain how Shelley's poem was an example of writing on the breath, each line a breath, each line brilliant poetry. Then he asked everyone to recite the poem, to breathe in before shouting each line. I stood in the back of the room trying to tolerate his eagerness, lack of self-consciousness and zeal to egg everyone on.

He proclaimed in a loud voice, "OH WILD WEST WIND!"

The students slowly, shyly responded until the room thundered with Allen's voice ringing out over the din:

> Thou, from whose unseen presence the leaves dead
> Are driven, like ghosts from an enchanter fleeing...

Stanza after stanza gathered momentum:

> Wild Spirit, which art moving everywhere;
> Destroyer and preserver; hear, oh, hear!

Each line a breath, finally an out-breath of stunning power. But I held back, put off by Allen's bellowing—his apparent foolish outrageousness.

This yearly event fell gratefully into my unconscious storehouse until a few years ago when I was wandering in Rome. I paid a visit to John Keats's apartment next to the Spanish Steps where he breathed his last. There was a portrait of Shelley sitting in the Roman Forum, which at the time of his visit in the early 1700s was still overgrown with vines. Transfixed, I gazed at the image, then looked out Keats's window to the Spanish Steps below packed with tourists and spiky-haired teenagers. It was Romantic, if you will. It was replete with impermanence, if you won't.

In a flash I grasped the struggles of the Romantic poets, their desire to find bone-warming passion, their Grand Tour devotion to the search for Western Civilization and beauty, their forays to the Eternal City. Later, in the now continually excavated Roman Forum, walking along the Via Sacra, I began to viscerally grasp what I had only known as lifeless albeit beautiful words on the page.

Circumstances found me back in the Roman Forum a month after Allen's death. Suddenly I heard his voice shouting "OH WILD WEST WIND!" A bookstore near the Spanish Steps had a copy of Shelley's poetry in English. Deep in the Roman Forum, atop Palatine Hill, looking out on the ruins of the Hippodrome, a plan took form. We would shout the *Ode* in the amphitheater of the ancestors of Western Civilization. Accompanied by my good friend and collaborator, Antonette, her 13-year-old son,

Zach, and his friend, Aaron—who continually complained: "We never walk in Boulder. We only walk on grass. Where's the car?"—we rallied to read the poem, to keep the breath new for each line:

> All overgrown with azure moss and flowers
> So sweet, the sense faints picturing them! Thou...

The boys faded a bit but we made it to the end. A while later, I shouted it again by myself:

> If I were a dead leaf thou mightest bear;
> If I were a swift cloud to fly with thee...

It didn't sound foolish or outrageous under the blue Mediterranean sky.

A year later, close to the first anniversary of his death, I was again in Rome. This time I was with my partner, Denny, and our 16-year-old godchild, Maron. We were in the enchanted Protestant Cemetery. We stood in the dappled sunlight at the foot of Shelley's grave and read from Xeroxed copies of the *Ode* that Cindy Carr, writer and dear friend (who journeyed with me to Naropa in 1976), had made for us while we stopped over in New York. The three of us, muses of Memory, Meditation and Song, read through to the end with gusto:

The Hippodrome on Palatine
Hill. Roman Forum. Roma.

Sweet though in sadness. Be thou, Spirit fierce,
My spirit! Be thou me, impetuous one!

Drive my dead thoughts over the universe
Like withered leaves to quicken a new birth!
And, by the incantation of this verse,

Scatter, as from an unextinguished hearth
Ashes and sparks, my words among mankind!
Be through my lips to unawakened earth

The trumpet of a prophecy! O, Wind,
If Winter comes, can Spring be far behind?

Allen was gone. Shelley and Keats were long gone. We were the living. The clover was green around Shelley's gravestone as it was when Allen plucked a few in the cemetery in the 1950s.[20] I didn't pick any. We could only send him our voices.

Was this simple recitation the unnoticed but powerful result of *darshan*? Had Allen taught me something while I was unawares? Certainly, I was willing to shout it, surrendering my self-consciousness in tribute to his volatile, still-illuminating and peregrine memory.

PERCY BYSSHE SHELLEY

COR CORDIUM

NATUS IVNIIG MDCCXCII

OBIIT VIII IVL MDCCC XXII

Shelley's grave high up against the wall of the Protestant Cemetery, Roma.

When we think of saints, we think of special people who suffered but were true to God no matter what befell them. We don't think of saints as ordinary people with nasty flaws. Saints are not like us. In this hagiographic attempt to grasp Allen's autobiographical lifestyle what makes him worthy of sainthood is that he was a human being resplendent with flaws. In spite of his failings, failings that he was all too conscious of, he passionately persisted in offering his best perceptions, his best language, his best voice.

Even hagiography is too limiting. If postmodern means to escape definitions that limit or impose arbitrary meaning, then Allen might be our man. If he was a Beat writer, then he went beyond the purely literary. If he was a champion of the First Amendment, he led the charge not just for himself but for anyone who was threatened by the enemies of free expression. If he was gay, his love was simple and immediate, "out" of the closet before it was a concept. If he was a teacher, his teaching encompassed poetics, Buddhism, history and simple but direct respect for the ancestors as well as the living practitioners.

He *was* saintly but he was also an ordinary teeth-flossing human being. If we consider him an autobiographical performance artist, we would only be describing a form he brought into prominence before it was prominent. We might conclude that postmodernism was inaugurated by his ubiquitous energies which filled the planet with passionate pure obscene sound. But more, we might be touched by his courage in the face of Moloch, his tenderness for the frailties of the human struggle to find meaning in life, love and work. Or we might give the next-to-last word to his mother, Naomi, as Allen did in *Kaddish*:[21]

> Strange Prophecies anew! She wrote—'The key is in the window, the
> key is in the sunlight at the window—I have the key—Get married Allen
> don't take drugs—the key is in the bars, in the sunlight in the window...'

Allen did marry. He married the word. He married the Buddha. He married the song. Allen married us. A merry-maker, in deed.

ALLEN GINSBERG
June 3, 1926—April 5, 1997

TYGER
7/10/92

Allen
Ginsberg
Naropa Institute

# AFTERWORD

When Judith Jerome invited me to do a piece about Allen Ginsberg for *Women & Performance/ A Journal of Feminist Theory,* published by Women & Performance Project, Inc., at New York University's Tisch School of the Arts, I was delighted. I hadn't seen Allen much in the years before his death and hadn't found a suitable way to acknowledge my appreciation and love for him.

The theme for this particular issue of *Women & Performance* was "Autobiography." Certainly Allen had used his life as material for his work, his work as material that informed his life. Since I had collaborated with Allen for many years and took a personal approach to our relationship, Judith perhaps saw an opportunity to get an unusual take on his life.

What take would that be? I wanted to include my personal perceptions of how autobiography played itself out in his life including how the Buddhist practice fit into the scheme. We were both practitioners. He was eager to see if *darshan* as a teaching practice would serve to join Western technique with Eastern path; I was curious to watch it all unfold and lend a hand when possible.

It took some time to do the piece since writing about Allen brought up a surfeit of feelings from laughter to bouts of grief. Our relationship often touched on deep intimacy. It also bounced along on the vagaries brought on by the ambition to establish a viable writing school outside of New York City. For all that we went through, good and not-so-good, writing the piece brought profound loss to the surface. It also brought relief because I could finally "pay tribute" to a great and generous man.

When Jennifer Heath offered to publish *The Wild West Wind/ Remembering Allen Ginsberg* with alterations and additions through Baksun Books, it meant the book would reach a wider audience of colleagues, former students and friends. She has included my illustrations, which brought together my long involvement in word, image and book arts. Allen was supportive of the Book Arts Program, which I founded with Barbara Bash at Naropa, especially when I told him that we were going to train students in the tradition of William Blake who designed, etched, printed and wrote his own works.

## ACKNOWLEDGEMENTS

First, let me thank my students who have taught me more than I can learn.

Thanks to Judith Jerome for her role as *deus ex machina*. Her vision provided a venue for a tribute to Allen. To Linda Nelson for the editorial care she took with the piece.

To Jennifer Heath for encouraging me to make the piece more widely available as well as to include my drawings. Admiration is boundless for her brilliance, generosity and patience.

Especially to C. Carr for our long friendship and for sharing her precious time—while she is finishing her own book—to write the introduction.

To Pat Donegan for the faculty photograph and her haiku practice. Her continuing support for my unconventional approach to the writer's path sustains me.

Gratitude to Steven Taylor who loaned Allen's harmonium so that I could draw it. In Steven's hands, it still emanates Allen's music love.

Allen's rendition of Blake's *Tyger* was generously loaned by Robert Morehouse.

Robert Morehouse, Gail Watson and Leslie Branton offered their professional Vermilion wisdom. Their design of the book jacket captures Allen's *modus operandi*.

Thanks to Laurie Price for spontaneous proof-reading.

To Michelle Visser for her technical expertise that helped finalize the manuscript.

To Brian Allen for his typographical knowledge of the computer age.

Thanks to Kess for bringing it to the finishline.

Appreciation always to Antonette Rosato for her patient, skillful and elegant design mind.

Kudos to the subscribers whose generous support provided the impetus to take on the demands of small press design and publication. And for your patience. May you enjoy the fruits of love's labor.

Deepest thanks to Denny Robertson for her unwavering expectation of a finished product, her fearless brilliance, golden love and sense of humor.

# A Note on the Illustrations

The illustrations began in Roma, Città Eterna, Bella Italia. Its awesome multi-layered beauty and history of the place revived my interest in pen-ink-drawing. The Hippodrome on Palatine Hill, the "collage" drawing of the Hippodrome and Shelley's grave were drawn *in situ*. The Hippodrome, a large stadium on the top of the hill, was chosen because I could imagine Allen proclaiming to large crowds in all his lifetimes. The composite drawing of the Hippodrome on the Notes page was drawn in Roman drizzle. Shelley's grave is in the magical Protestant Cemetery in Rome. It's high up against the wall that surrounds the cemetery. Cats, cared for by a society of ladies of London, frolic and brush up against you. Flowers bloom and gravestones carry elaborate tales of the dearly-departeds' undying love for Rome.

The empty chair under the tree on the Naropa campus is my last memory of Allen.

The drawing of Allen, Anne and Gregory is from an archival photo from the 1970s, the Age of Hair.

Chögyam Trungpa Rinpoche's likeness is based on a 1983 archival photo taken at Karma Chöling in Vermont.

The cover drawing of Allen is from an old photograph I have in my collection, photographer unknown.

Shelley sitting in the Roman Forum is from a postcard of Joseph Severn's 1845 painting of same purchased at the Keats-Shelley Memorial House on the Spanish Steps in Rome. Severn is buried next to Shelley.

*The School of Athens* provides an ancestral backdrop for Allen's conversations with Blake. Perhaps it is a stretch to overlay Aristotle and Plato with these two poets, but I couldn't resist the palimpsest theme that is so much a part of Allen's poetics.

The faux heraldry drawing on the title page I created for Allen's birthday in the early 1980s. He was a tiger then only to later metamorphose into a Dharma Lion.

The Millennial Calligraphy on the end papers is a practice of writing that I began in an effort to heal some blockages in my life that couldn't be put into words. Born left-handed, I like to write from right to left. It is physically relaxing and easier to do than struggle with the right-handed practice. This kind of writing has made its appearance on more than one of my pieces even as it began as a private study and way of working with calligraphy, a practice taught to me by my father when I was a wee one.

Faculty gathering early 1980s in the backyard of Pat's and my house, 1021 Grant Place. Standing left to right: Dick Gallup, Susan Edwards, Pat Donegan, JoAnne Kyger, Michael Brownstein. Kneeling knights: Peter Orlovsky and Allen Ginsberg.

CLOUDY SKY CHILL SETS IN
SHELLEY SAYS "YOU'RE
NOT ALONE." I CRY CROSSING
THE STEET TO PIRAMIDE LOOKS
LIKE RAIN IN THE SKY AS WELL

## NOTES

1. Chögyam Trungpa Rinpoche, (1937-1987), a meditation master and Tibetan refugee, established his first U.S. practice center in Barnet, Vermont. In the early 1970s, he made Boulder his main center. Here he founded Vajradhatu, an international organization now led by his son, the Sakyong, Mipam Rinpoche. The organization includes Shambhala Training, Naropa Institute (now Naropa University), Rocky Mountain Dharma Center (now Rocky Mountain Shambhala Center), Mudra Theatre Group and Ashoka Credit Union among others. While the "capital" moved to Halifax, Nova Scotia, Canada,

Boulder is still a large and thriving center that attracts Tibetan Buddhist lamas, artists and writers to teach and continue their work.

2. See Nicosia, Gerald. 1992. "The Beat of His Own Drums."

3. Ginsberg. 1984. *Allen Ginsberg, Collected Poems 1947-1980*, page 129.

4. Ibid. 1984, page 146.

5. Smith, Dinitia. 1996. "How Allen Ginsberg Thinks his Thoughts."

6. Ginsberg. 1980. *Composed on the Tongue, Literary Conversation*, 1967-1977, page 8.

7. Ibid., page 16. The Buddhist Three Vows are conventionally referred to as the Refuge Prayer: "I take refuge in the Buddha, I take refuge in the Dharma, I take refuge in the Sangha." One is accepting three things: the possibility that a human being can achieve enlightenment as the Buddha did; that the teachings are essential to the path; that fellow practitioners are heart-comrades.

8. See Allen's Foreword to *The Beat Book*, page xiv.

9. Although it took determination, Pat Donegan finally got Ginsberg's respect and blessing when he realized she was a legitimate part of the Williams-Imagist-haiku lineage. She also began, under his tutelage, to write longer poems in a stronger style and it impressed Allen that Chögyam Trungpa Rinpoche requested that Pat compose poems on the spot as he did with Allen. Finally, Allen wrote a foreword and a book-blurb for Donegan's collection of poems, *Without Warning*. They were colleagues at Naropa from 1976 to 1985.

10. Varsity Apartments, 1515 Broadway, was the apartment complex that Naropa rented during the summer months for visiting faculty and students. Its central courtyard provided an intimacy and an inescapable whirlpool of high jinks and "creative" passions.

11. Gregory Corso, March 26, 1930—January 19, 2001.  As the book was almost completed, Gregory Corso died. Tom Peters organized a reading of his poetry at Penny Lane Coffee House in Boulder. Colleagues, former students and old friends read selections from his work. Reed Bye, Peter Michelson, Randy Roark, Jim Cohn, Sue Rhynhart, Todd Pinney, Tom Peters, Jane and Bataan Faigao, Joe Richey and myself were among the readers. It was a cold blustery night. (Alas, a few weeks later, Jane Faigao shrugged off her mortal coil.)

Gregory's ashes are interred in the Protestant Cemetery in Rome. Even though Gregory was an Italian-American Catholic, he was an irascible Protest-ant. Surely the Italians, who are fond of him, will accept his choice to be with his beloved Shelley and Keats. May their ashes co-mingle and Gregory's lyrical voice remain with us for a long time.

12. Lincoln, Andrew, ed. 1965. *William Blake songs of Innocence and Experience*. Vol. 2, plate 43.

13. Ginsberg, 1970. *Indian Journals*, page 154.

14. Ginsberg, 1984. *Collected Poems 1947-1980*, page 781, note 435.

15. Donegan, Pat. 1997. "A Homage to Allen Ginsberg and His Haiku."

16. See Bibliography for a selection of Chögyam Trungpa Rinpoche's poetry books.

17. For more information on Norman Podhoretz's neo-conservative opinion of Allen, see his book, *Ex-Friends, Falling out with Allen Ginsberg, Lionel and Diana Trilling, Lillian Hellman, Hannah Arendt, and Norman Mailer*, pages 22-56. On a recent C-Span literary panel, Podhoretz opined that Allen was "evil."

18. Gittings, R., ed. 1970. *The Letters of John Keats: A Selection*, page 43. Keats' notion of negative capability pops up in such disparate places as social research and in the talk of pop rockers.

19. Hutchinson, Thomas, ed. 1965. *The Complete Poems of Percy Bysshe Shelley,* page 577.

In Shelley's "Defense of Poetry" (1821), he places poets above philosophers in their influence. Civilization is the result of poetry that teaches man "moral improvement" not by teaching moral doctrine but by enlarging the power of imagination by which man puts himself "in the place of another." Poets are the "unacknowledged legislators of the world." See more about this in *The New Princeton Encyclopedia of Poetry and Poetics,* pages 1086-87.

20. Ball, Gordon, ed. 1995. *Allen Ginsberg: Journals Mid-Fifties, 1954-1958,* page 369.

21. Ginsberg. 1984, page 224.

# SELECTED BIBLIOGRAPHY

Ball, Gordon, ed. 1995. *Allen Ginsberg: Journals Mid-Fifties, 1954-1958*. HarperCollins: NY.

Carr, C. 1993. *On Edge: performance at the end of the twentieth century*. Wesleyan University Press, Hanover: NH. A collection of essays that appeared in the *Village Voice, Artforum* and the *L.A. Weekly*.

Donegan, Pat and Ishibashi, Yoshie. 1998. *Chiyo-ni: Woman Haiku Master*. Tuttle: Tokyo. A collaborative translation of an 18th century poet.

Donegan, Pat, 1997. "A Homage to Allen Ginsberg and His Haiku" *Frogpond*. XX:1, Haiku Society of America: NY.

—1990. *Without Warning Poems* by Patricia Donegan. Foreword by Allen Ginsberg. Parallax Press: CA.

—1985. *Bone Poems (Mini-Cantos)*. Chinook Press: Boulder.

—1980. *Never mind*. Edited by Patricia Donegan and Jim Cohn. Kokoro Press: Boulder.

Erdman, David V., ed. 1965. *The Poetry and Prose of William Blake*. Doubleday: NY.

Ginsberg, Allen. 1984. *Allen Ginsberg, Collected Poems 1947-1980*. Harper and Row: NY.

—1980. *Composed on the Tongue, Literary Conversation*, 1967-1977. Grey Fox Press: Bolinas.

—1970. *Indian Journals.* Dan Haselwood Books and City Lights Books: San Francisco.

Hutchinson, Thomas, ed. 1965. *The Complete Poems of Percy Bysshe Shelley.* Oxford.

Jerome, Judith and Satin, Leslie, eds. 1999. Women & Performance/a journal of feminist theory. "Performing Autobiography." Volume 10:1-2, #19-20. Tisch School of the Arts, New York University, NY.

Lincoln, Andrew, ed. 1965. *William Blake songs of Innocence and Experience.* Vol. 2. The William Blake Trust/Princeton University Press: NJ.

Joyce, James. 1986. *Ulysses: The Corrected Text.* Vintage: NY.

Nicosia, Gerald. 1992. "The Beat of His Own Drums." Book Review, *Los Angeles Times*, Nov. 29.

Podhoretz, Norman. 1999. *Ex-Friends: Falling Out with Allen Ginsberg, Lionel & Diana Trilling, Lillian Hellman, Hannah Arendt, and Norman Mailer.* The Free Press, a division of Simon and Schuster: NY.

Preminger, Alex and Brogan, T. V. F., eds. 1993. *The New Princeton Encyclopedia of Poetry and Poetics.* Princeton University Press, Princeton: NJ.

Rosenthal, Bob, Peter Hale and Bill Morgan, eds. 1999. *Allen Ginsberg: Death & Fame, Poems 1993-1997.* HarperFlamingo, HarperCollins: NY.

Sanders, Ed. 1993-94. *The Fugs First Album*, reissued as ESP 1018, Fantasy Records, Berkeley: CA. A fantastic rendition of William Blake's *Ah! Sunflower.*

Schumacher, Michael. 1992. *Dharma Lion: A Critical Biography of Allen Ginsberg.* St. Martin's Press: NY.

Skau, Michael. 1999. *"A Clown in a Grave" Complexities and Tensions in the Works of Gregory Corso*. Southern Illinois University Press: IL. A timely, critical look at Gregory Corso's poetry and outlook.

Smith, Dinitia. 1996. "How Allen Ginsberg Thinks his Thoughts." *New York Times*, Oct. 8.

Trungpa, Chögyam. 1998. *Timely Rain: selected poetry of Chögyam Trungpa*. Foreword: Allen Ginsberg. Shambhala: Boston.

—1995. *Royal Songs*. Trident Publications. Halifax: Canada.

—1983, *First Thought, Best Thought: 108 Poems*. Introduction by Allen Ginsberg. Shambhala: Boston.

Waldman, Anne, ed. 1996. *The Beat Book*. Foreword by Allen Ginsberg. Shambhala Books: Boston.

Whitman, Walt. 1982. *Walt Whitman: Complete Poetry and Collected Prose*. The Library of America: NY.

Williams, William Carlos. 1946. *Paterson (Book One)*. New Directions: CA.

Susan Edwards is a writer, book artist and metaphysician. She taught writing, sacred literature and did collaborative performance at Naropa University from 1979 to 1990 where she co-founded the Book Arts Program with Barbara Bash and directed the undergraduate Writing and Poetics Department. In her current work, she seeks to bring images and text together in aesthetic and digital ways. She also has her own company, **THE PRACTICAL MYSTIC,** that produces and distributes tapes, chapbooks, broadsides and offers lectures and sometimes classes.

 **THE PRACTICAL MYSTIC**

# Colophon

This book is a collaborative effort between **BAKSUN BOOKS** and **THE PRACTICAL MYSTIC.** It was designed by Susan Edwards on Quark with Photoshop. Jennifer Heath brought her publisher's vision to the project. Vermilion contributed design and technical support. Typeface is Cloister. Seven hundred and fifty copies printed on Mohawk Superfine paper and endpapers on Glama Translucent by PIP Printers in Boulder.

## OTHER BOOKS BY BAKSUN BOOKS

*La Niña: Urban Fairy Tales*, comix by Sarah C. Bell
*On the Way Here*, stories by Tree Bernstein
*The Task*, poems by Jack Collom
*First Presence*, stories by Jane Wodening
*Where Hunger is a Place: 14 Sonnets*, by Laura Wright

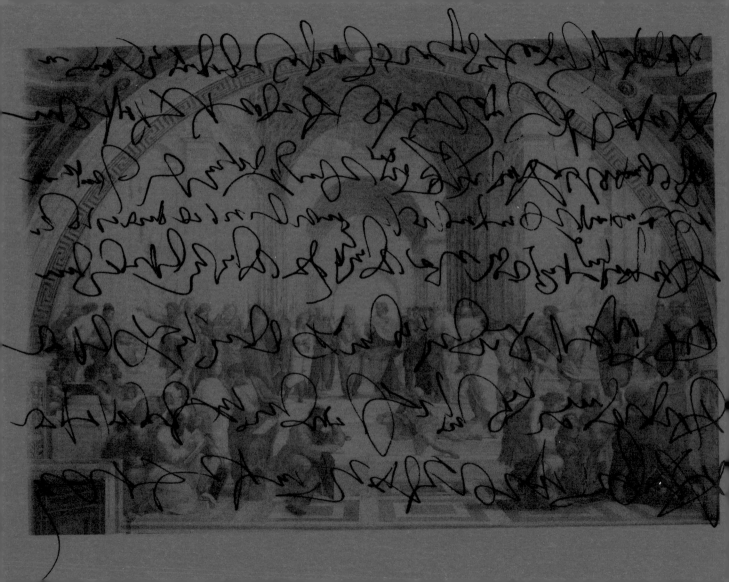